# God is Not Mad at You

# at You

# He's Madly in Love

# with You

by

## AL JENNINGS

Joann,
Jesus is
proud of you!

2016

Bonus
Grace Roundtable Video

As a way of saying thank you for your purchase, I want to give you a free video download. Pull up a chair and listen in as I discuss the gospel of grace with NFL sports agents Eugene Parker and Roosevelt Barnes.

Here's the link to your video: http://aljennings.com/grace
Enjoy!

# Table of Contents

God is Not Mad at You

He's Madly in Love with You

# Introduction

The gospel is good news. Unfortunately, there is misinformation being spread by well-meaning Christians that presents God as a mean, intolerant bully who is ready to swat you with a giant fly swatter when you make a mistake. The word *gospel* means good news. Therefore, if you hear a message about God that is not good news, it is not the gospel. Jesus went around doing good (Acts 10:38). God wants His goodness to lead us to repentance (Romans 2:4).

If you look at the news, you may notice that Christians are oftentimes shown as people who are mean and dogmatic. This is not the message of Jesus. And this is not the message of the cross. The message of the Bible is love and acceptance. Jesus did not go around condemning people. He loved people.

God's motive is love. Love is the driving force behind everything He does. He does not put bad things on you to teach you lessons. When you see the true God of the Bible, I am convinced that you will want to put your trust in Him. He wants to do good things for you. Jesus came so you could live the abundant life. He died on the cross to be kind to you. He demonstrated His love for you by His death on the cross.

Religion has misrepresented God. Many churches and religions have caused people to feel as if God is mad at them. They feel that God is condemning, harsh, unforgiving, cruel, and judgmental. Although religion has presented Him as such, that is not God's nature. There is something in you that knows that God cannot be the way religion has presented Him. I want you to know that God is not mad at you. He is madly in love with you and that is what this book is all about, God's good opinion of you.

The devil likes to trick people into believing lies about God that are not based on the Bible to keep them in bondage. The devil wants you to think that God is a tyrannical ruler who cannot be trusted, and that He is always looking to punish you for every infraction. That is a doctrine the devil started, and he has been promoting that lie ever since the Garden of Eden. He is a liar and the author of confusion (John 8:44; 1 Corinthians 14:33). He has been lying and confusing mankind for a very long time, and he is very good at it. It takes the light of God's Word to expose him. When you get a revelation of God's Word, you will not be ignorant of the devil's schemes (2 Corinthians 2:11). I am confident that once you understand God's true character and receive what He has for you, you will start winning in life.

Matthew 7:11 (NKJV)
11 If you then, being evil, know how to give good gifts to your children, how much more will your Father who is in heaven give good things to those who ask Him!

God is our Father and He has good things in store for us. If you are a parent, you want the best for your children. You know within yourself that something is wrong with a Father who is always looking to punish his children for their mistakes. God is not a cruel dictator with a giant fly swatter. This is the reason why many people stay away from church. They believe in God, but they have a problem with church because of the way the Church has presented God.

Some churches teach that God does not want you to have success, and it is wrong for you to be prosperous because it is the root of all evil. Some even suggest God wants you to be poor, and they try to make you feel guilty for being prosperous. That is not the God of the Bible. You do not have to give all of your money away to serve God. Jesus was made to be poor that we might be rich (2 Corinthians 8:9).

Joshua 1:8 (NKJV)
8 This Book of the Law shall not depart from your mouth, but you shall meditate in it day and night, that you may observe to do according to all that is written in it. For then you will make your way prosperous, and then you will have good success.

Psalm 1:3 (NCV)
3 They are strong, like a tree planted by a river. The tree produces fruit in season, and its leaves don't die. Everything they do will succeed.

God wants you to be prosperous. Solomon was wealthy. Abraham was wealthy. God is for you. He wants you to succeed.

John 10:10 (NLT)
10 The thief's purpose is to steal and kill and destroy. My purpose is to give them a rich and satisfying life.

God wants to enhance your life. He wants to make your life beautiful, wonderful and fruitful. God wants you to have fun and enjoy life. He is not a taker; He is a giver. Jesus wants you to have an abundant life. God is not a mean bully. He is a good God and His mercy endures forever. He is a loving and kind heavenly God who wants to have an intimate relationship with you. I want to introduce you to the God of the Bible. If you want God without religion, this book is for you.

# CHAPTER ONE

## *Why Bad Things Happen*

There are people who hear some Christians say that God is in control of the world. So, they ask questions like, if God is in control of this world, why is it in such a mess? Why does He not do something about all the inequalities and injustices in the world? Why does He not do something to stop all the wars in the world? Why did He not do something about those planes crashing into the World Trade Center on Sept. 11? Why does He not do something to stop the senseless killings that go on in the world? Let us look into why bad things happen in the world.

2 Corinthians 4:4 (KJV)
4 In whom the god of this world hath blinded the minds of them which believe not, lest the light of the glorious gospel of Christ, who is the image of God, should shine unto them.

Satan is referenced, in 2 Corinthians 4:4, as the "god of this world."

Genesis 1:26 (NKJV)
Then God said, "Let Us make man in Our image, according to Our likeness; let them have dominion over the fish of the sea,

over the birds of the air, and over the cattle, over all the earth and over every creeping thing that creeps on the earth."

In the garden, God gave Adam the dominion or authority of this world. Adam was the (little g) god of this world. Then how did Satan become the god of this world? The temptation of Jesus in the wilderness gives us insight into this.

Luke 4:5-8 (NKJV)
Then the devil, taking Him up on a high mountain, showed Him all the kingdoms of the world in a moment of time. And the devil said to Him, "All this authority I will give You, and their glory; for this has been delivered to me, and I give it to whomever I wish. Therefore, if You will worship before me, all will be Yours." And Jesus answered and said to him, "Get behind Me, Satan! For it is written, 'You shall worship the LORD your God, and Him only you shall serve.' "

The devil tempted Jesus and told Him, "All this authority I will give You..." The authority he is talking about is the authority of the kingdoms of the world. He went on to tell Jesus, "...and I give it to whomever I wish." The authority of this world belonged to Satan. He had the right to offer the kingdoms of the world to anyone he wanted. Satan obtained the authority of this world when Adam ate from the tree of the knowledge of good and evil in the Garden of Eden. By doing so, he turned the authority and dominion of this world over to Satan. Satan became the (little g) god of this world. This was a legal transaction and Satan has been in charge ever since.

It is like a person who rents an apartment. He does not own the apartment, but he has a right to put furniture in the apartment and arrange the apartment any way he pleases. The owner just cannot barge in anytime he wants, sit down in the renter's living room and watch TV. He has to abide by the rules of the contract. God is in ultimate authority and control of this world, but Satan has a temporary lease on the world. Satan has a right to be here until his lease runs out. He is the one who is responsible for the evil, not God. Eventually, his lease will run out and God will take back control. Until then, God cannot do anything about the evil in the world. He has the power, but He does not have the right. Satan has a legal lease. And since God is a just God, He will not violate the lease agreement.

James 1:13 (NKJV)
13 Let no one say when he is tempted, "I am tempted by God"; for God cannot be tempted by evil, nor does He Himself tempt anyone.

When bad things happen, God is not responsible. He does not tempt anyone with evil things. Temptations, trials, and tests come from the wicked one. He is the one who steals, kills, and destroys.

## The Believer Has Authority Over All the Devil's Power

John 10:10 (NKJV)
10 The thief does not come except to steal, and to kill, and to destroy. I have come that they may have life, and that they may have it more abundantly.

Satan's purpose is to steal, kill, and destroy. Jesus came to give us abundant life. Although Satan has authority in the world, he has no authority over the believer in Christ. When Jesus went to the cross, He defeated Satan (Colossians 2:14–15). All authority in heaven and earth was given to Jesus (Matthew 28:18). Jesus gave the believer authority over all the devil's power.

Luke 10:19 (NKJV)
19 Behold, I give you the authority to trample on serpents and scorpions, and over all the power of the enemy, and nothing shall by any means hurt you.

The Bible never tells us to fight the Devil. It says cast him out (Mark 16:17), give him no place (Ephesians 4:27), resist him (James 4:7), and trample on him. The reason why we do not have to fight the Devil is because Jesus whipped him on the cross. Do not be afraid of the Devil, because he is a defeated foe. Sickness and lack come from the enemy. He has no right to put those things on you. So, when he tries to attack your finances or your health, use your authority over him.

## The Way of Escape

1 Corinthians 10:13 (NKJV)
13 No temptation has overtaken you except such as is common to man; but God is faithful, who will not allow you to be tempted beyond what you are able, but with the temptation will also make the way of escape, that you may be able to bear it.

The trials of life come to us all, but they do not come from God. God is the one who gives us the way of escape. It would not make sense for God to be the one who is tempting us and then turn around and gives us the way of escape.

James 1:17 (NKJV)
17 Every good gift and every perfect gift is from above, and comes down from the Father of lights, with whom there is no variation or shadow of turning.

Bad things do not come from God; they come from Satan. God only has good things for you. Satan is the source of all the problems in world. He is the one who tries to make our lives miserable, not God.

# CHAPTER TWO
## *It's Already Done*

When I was a kid, I remember watching *Gilligan's Island* when I came home from school. The show was about seven people stranded on an island. On the show, there was a Japanese character who randomly showed up from time to time. He had been a soldier in World War II, which had ended, but nobody had told him the war was over.

I learned recently that his character was based on a true story about a man named Hiroo Onada. For 29 years, he was isolated on a small Philippine island because he thought that World War II was going on when actually it was over. Several times the Japanese government sent messages to try to persuade him that the war was over. He dismissed the messages as enemy propaganda and refused to believe them.

Finally, Onada surrendered and came home to a hero's welcome. For 29 years, this man fought a war that only existed in his mind. His commitment was commendable but unnecessary.

This is like many Christians today. They think that God is angry with them because of their sins. God is no longer angry with man because of man's sins. While that was true in the Old Testament, it is not true anymore because Jesus was punished for sins on the cross. Because of that, the war between God and man is over. On the cross, Jesus ended the war between God and man.

John 19:30 (NKJV)
30 So when Jesus had received the sour wine, He said, "It is finished!" And bowing His head, He gave up His spirit.

When Jesus was on the cross He said, "It is finished". What He was referring to was the Old Testament law. Jesus fulfilled the law. We have now died to the law and are now married to Jesus (Romans 7:4). We have a new and better covenant established upon better promises (Hebrews 8:6).

The new covenant is all about God doing and us resting. We are back to the Garden of Eden where God rested on the seventh day after creating the earth in six days (Genesis 2:2). It does not mean that God was tired after six days and then took a well-deserved nap. After all, creating the whole world is a pretty big deal. He looked over everything He had made and saw "It was good." (Genesis 1:31) When God saw it was good, He meant perfect. In fact, creation was so good that nothing has been created since then.

Rest does not imply exhaustion. Rest means complete or done. When the Bible says that God rested, it means that God ceased from activity. He completed the work. His work was finished. It is the same as when a lawyer finishes defending his case and says the defense rests. He is saying he is done. Or, when an artist finishes his painting and feels that another stroke would ruin it, he does not paint another stroke. He is done.

All Adam had to do after God finished His work was to reach out, receive what God had already done, and say, "Thank you." That is an example for us today of how to walk in the new covenant. God did all the work by sending Jesus. "It is finished" means that the work was completed. It was a finished work. We are to simply rest in the finished work of Jesus on the cross. We just receive it and say, "Thank you, Father; thank you, Jesus!"

## The Cross Was a Rescue Mission

Jesus' going to the cross was a rescue mission to bring man back to God. Jesus' job description is a savior. He redeemed us by taking our place, dying on the cross, and taking the punishment for our sin.

2 Corinthians 5:21 (NKJV)
21 For He made Him who knew no sin to be sin for us, that we might become the righteousness of God in Him.

The Bible is the greatest love story ever told. It is a redemption story about God bringing man back to Himself. It is as if they put out an Amber alert for a child that is missing. The family and everyone close to them go all out and do everything in their power to look for and rescue the child. They put out flyers, alert the authorities, and do whatever they can.

That is what God did in sending Jesus. He came after us with everything He had. He warned the devil shortly after Adam sinned that the woman's (Mary) offspring (Jesus) would crush his head (Genesis 3:15). And He did this by sending Jesus. God would do anything for us. Romans 8:32 tells us that since He did not spare His own Son, He surely will give us everything else we need.

Matthew 1:21 (NLT)
21 And she will have a son, and you are to name him Jesus, for he will save his people from their sins.

The old covenant was a law-based system based on rules of do's and don'ts. But Jesus ushered in another system that is not based on rules. (John 1:17) Moses gave us the law, which included the "Big Ten" Commandments. Jesus came to save us. The cross was a rescue mission. Jesus' job description is a savior. We were drowning and Jesus rescued us. When you are drowning, you do not need somebody to throw you a book on how to swim. You need someone to jump in and save you. That is what Jesus did for us!

Ephesians 1:3 (NKJV)

3 Blessed be the God and Father of our Lord Jesus Christ, who has blessed us with every spiritual blessing in the heavenly places in Christ,

Notice the past tense of God's Word. This verse says, "...has blessed us." These spiritual blessings have already been given.

Spiritual blessings are not just things we cannot touch like joy or peace. They include those things, but they also include things like healing and finances. Spiritual blessings are blessings that proceed from the spirit realm, which include earthly blessings.

2 Peter 1:3–4 (NKJV)

3 as His divine power has given to us all things that pertain to life and godliness, through the knowledge of Him who called us by glory and virtue,

4 by which have been given to us exceedingly great and precious promises, that through these you may be partakers of the divine nature, having escaped the corruption that is in the world through lust.

Here again in Peter, we see the past tense used in reference to the promises of God.

Healing and prosperity pertain to life. Second Corinthians 1:20 says that all the promises of God are yes and amen. The promises are yes because they were provided for us through the finished work of Jesus on the cross. These promises include healing and prosperity. By His stripes, we were healed (1 Peter 2:24). Jesus was made to be poor that we could be rich (2 Corinthians 8:9).

What do you do to be born again? Do you have to earn it or work for it? No. Why? You do not earn it or work for it because the price has already been paid for your salvation through the finished work of Jesus on the cross. Salvation is totally by grace through believing and not of self-effort (Ephesians 2:8-9). So, all that is left for you to do is receive what Jesus has purchased for us at Calvary.

On the cross, Jesus said that it is finished; not that it has started. You did not work for your salvation, so you do not have to work for anything else, like your healing or prosperity.

# CHAPTER THREE

## *The Difference Between Law and Grace*

John 1:17 (NKJV)
17 For the law was given through Moses, but grace and truth came through Jesus Christ.

The Old Testament law is not the gospel. The law came through Moses, but grace and truth came through Jesus Christ. Notice that truth is on the side of grace, not on the side of the law. Grace is God's unmerited favor. Jesus is grace personified. Jesus did not come to give us a set of rules. Jesus is not a lawgiver but a savior.

Under the law, the blessings of God were based on obeying the commandments. The new covenant is all about Jesus obeying the commandments and dying on the cross on our behalf. He was the only one who could keep the law perfectly. The law will only point out your faults but it will not lift a finger to help. The good news is that Jesus fulfilled the law on our behalf (Matthew 5:17). He became what we were so we could become who He is. Today, we stand complete in Him (Colossians 2:10). We are the righteousness of God in Christ Jesus (2 Corinthians 5:21).

Hebrews 8: 8-10, 12 (NKJV)
8 ... I will make a new covenant with the house of Israel and with the house of Judah—

9 not according to the covenant that I made with their fathers....
10 ...I will put My laws in their mind and write them on their hearts; and I will be their God, and they shall be My people....
12 For I will be merciful to their unrighteousness, and their sins and their lawless deeds I will remember no more."

The gospel is not a set of do's and don'ts. The language of the law is do. The language of grace is done. The language of the law is you shall not. The language of the cross is "I will." Notice how many times "I will" is mentioned. The "I" refers to God.

**Understanding the Purpose of the Law**

Galatians 3:24–25 (NKJV)
24 Therefore the law was our tutor to bring us to Christ, that we might be justified by faith.
25 But after faith has come, we are no longer under a tutor.

The law was never intended to make us right with God. The law was given to bring us to the end of ourselves and show us that we need a savior. Its purpose was to point us to Jesus. The law was our tutor to bring us to Christ. Now that we have Christ, we are no longer under the tutor of the law.

Have you ever taken a mirror from the wall and tried to fix your hair with it? Of course not! The law is like a mirror. It can show you a pimple on your face, but it cannot remove it. The law will never encourage you. It will just show you where you fall short.

Hebrews 10:1–3 (NLT)

1 The old system under the law of Moses was only a shadow, a dim preview of the good things to come, not the good things themselves. The sacrifices under that system were repeated again and again, year after year, but they were never able to provide perfect cleansing for those who came to worship.

2 If they could have provided perfect cleansing, the sacrifices would have stopped, for the worshipers would have been purified once for all time, and their feelings of guilt would have disappeared.

3 But instead, those sacrifices actually reminded them of their sins year after year.

The law required animal sacrifices that were offered for the sins of the people. They were brought to the high priest year after year on behalf of the people to atone for their sins. They had to be brought continually because they could never take away sins. These animals were types of Jesus.

Hebrews 9:12 (NKJV)

12 Not with the blood of goats and calves, but with His own blood He entered the Most Holy Place once for all, having obtained eternal redemption.

Hebrews 10:12 (NKJV)

12 But this Man, after He had offered one sacrifice for sins forever, sat down at the right hand of God,

Jesus was the final sacrifice that ended the Old Testament law. When Jesus went to the cross, He said, "It is finished" (John 19:30). There are no more sacrifices because Jesus' final sacrifice brought perfect cleansing. Our sins have been removed as far as the East is from the West (Psalm 103:12). Our sins have been cancelled once and for all through the sacrifice of Jesus. Notice that Hebrews 10:12 says Jesus offered one sacrifice for "sins forever". *Sins forever* means that our past, present, and future sins have been forgiven. That is the gospel. That is the good news. Sin should not even be on our radar. We have been set free from sin. Sin shall not have dominion over us because we are not under the law but under grace (Romans 6:14).

Hebrews 8:10 (NKJV)

10 For this is the covenant that I will make with the house of Israel after those days, says the Lord: I will put My laws in their mind and write them on their hearts; and I will be their God, and they shall be My people.

In the new covenant, God gave us the Holy Spirit and the Spirit has written God's laws on our hearts.

The Holy Spirit is a living person who lives on the inside of us to be our helper. He wants to have an intimate relationship with us. We are to be led and instructed by the Holy Spirit, not the Ten Commandments. He will teach us all things (John 14:26) and guide us in life.

## God Did What the Law Could Not Do

Romans 8:3 (NKJV)
For what the law could not do in that it was weak through the flesh, God did by sending His own Son in the likeness of sinful flesh, on account of sin: He condemned sin in the flesh,

One day when I was reading this verse, the words, "God did," jumped out at me. God did what the law could not do, which is to make us right with God.

There was not anything wrong with the law. However, there was something wrong with us. We were weak because of our flesh. We were unable to keep the law. The law put a "Band-Aid" on sin, but did not remove it.

So, God in His mercy, demonstrated His own (perfect) love for us (Romans 5:8), and sent Jesus in the likeness of our flesh, as an offering for sin. He condemned sin in Jesus' flesh. Sin was judged in the body of Jesus.

Jesus took our place and became like we were to make us right with God. Because of Jesus, we are righteous **now**.

## God Does Not Look at Us When We Sin

Hebrews 10:2 (NKJV)
2 For then would they not have ceased to be offered? For the worshipers, once purified, would have had no more consciousness of sins.

In the Old Testament when they brought the lamb, the priest had to examine it to make sure that it was perfect. He did not examine the person bringing the sacrifice; he examined the lamb. The priest did not say to the person, "Let me make sure you are truly sorry for your sins."

They had to continue bringing sacrifices under the Old Testament because the sacrifices were animals. Because Jesus was a perfect sacrifice, He only had to offer Himself once. His once-and-for-all sacrifice made us perfect forever. The old system of sacrifices has stopped because we have been forgiven for all our sins – past, present, and future.

As an act of identification, the person bringing the sacrifice had to place his hands on the lamb. That was symbolic of his sins being transferred to the animal.

Listen carefully because this is a powerful truth. Once you get a revelation of it, you will be free from guilt and condemnation forever.

Jesus is our lamb who took away the sins of the world (John 1:29). Our sins were transferred to Jesus, and Jesus' righteousness was imparted to us. When we sin, God does not examine us to see if we have really repented, He examines the sacrifice at His right hand, who is perfect.

You may say, "But we do not deserve righteousness." You are right. I have a question for you, "Did Jesus deserve to be made sin (2 Corinthians 5:21)?" No. The cross was an exchange, our sin for Jesus' righteousness. He got what He did not deserve, so we could get what we did not deserve.

Since the perfect lamb made one sacrifice for sins for all time, God does not look at us to judge us when we sin. He looks at the sacrifice who has already been judged.

That is why God said that He would never be angry with us or rebuke us. He will neither stop showing kindness to us nor remove His covenant of peace from us (Isaiah 54:7–9). Our Father will never stop loving and being good to us (Jeremiah 32:40).

The devil will try to make you feel guilty and unworthy to ask God for anything. When the enemy tries to make you feel ashamed to approach God's throne, say aloud that you are the righteousness of God in Christ Jesus. When you confess your righteousness, you are agreeing with what God says about you. You are who God says you are no matter what anyone else says.

God does not want you to live with a consciousness of sin. As you renew your mind to who you are in Christ and to your righteousness, you will develop a righteousness consciousness. Whenever you have thoughts of guilt or shame, remind yourself of your righteousness.

So, come boldly to God's throne and receive whatever you need or desire from Him. Regardless of what you have done or what mistakes you have made, God does not look at you; He looks at the sacrifice. And the sacrifice is perfect. We are identified with the sacrifice, so we are perfect (Hebrews 10:14). As He is, so are we in this world (1 John 4:17). Praise God!

## Paid in Full

Let us say you owed Macy's department store $1,000 and I walked in, went to the accounting department, and paid all of your debt. Also, I told them to charge any future purchases for the rest of your life to my account. Would you continue to make monthly payments after I paid your debt in full? That would be foolish. Why? Because the debt has already been paid. Not only those but any future charges you will ever make for as long as you live have already been paid. That would be great news.

Well, I have better news. That is what Jesus did about your sins. He offered one sacrifice for sins forever. Why would you want to try to pay for something that has already been paid? Jesus' finished work on the cross paid for your sins for all time - past, present, and future. All you need to do is say, "Thank you". Your sins have already been paid. All the sins for your entire life have already been taken care of - paid in full! This happened on the cross when Jesus said, "It is finished" (John 19:30)!

Rest assured that God is not punishing you for your sins today. He is not holding any of His blessings back from you because of something you have done wrong. You are not experiencing bad things because God is punishing you for your sins. Do not misunderstand me; God does not like sin, and I am not saying that you should go out and sin all you want because you are forgiven. What I am saying is your sins are not making God angry with you.

# CHAPTER FOUR

## *What is the New Covenant?*

Hebrews 8:8–12 (NKJV)

8 Because finding fault with them, He says: "Behold, the days are coming, says the Lord, when I will make a new covenant with the house of Israel and with the house of Judah—9 not according to the covenant that I made with their fathers in the day when I took them by the hand to lead them out of the land of Egypt; because they did not continue in My covenant, and I disregarded them, says the Lord. 10 For this is the covenant that I will make with the house of Israel after those days, says the Lord: I will put My laws in their mind and write them on their hearts; and I will be their God, and they shall be My people. 11 None of them shall teach his neighbor, and none his brother, saying, 'Know the Lord,' for all shall know Me, from the least of them to the greatest of them. 12 For I will be merciful to their unrighteousness, and their sins and their lawless deeds I will remember no more."

Today we are living in the new covenant dispensation of grace. We are no longer under the Old Testament law.

The word *for* in verse 12 means "because." The reason why God can write His laws in our hearts and put them on our minds, the reason He can be our God, and the reason why all will know Him are because He will be merciful to our unrighteousness, and our sins and lawless deeds He remembers no more.

The reason He does not remember our sins is because Jesus was judged on the cross for our sins and the sins of the whole world. Jesus took our sins past, present, and future when He died on the cross.

God does not remember our sins anymore. Praise God; hallelujah! And that, my friend, is the new covenant. That is good news! That is over the top good news! That is the gospel!

So, what is our responsibility in this new covenant of grace? It is simply to believe. We are to believe that we are already forgiven and depend on that forgiveness every day. There is no condemnation or judgment to those who are in Christ Jesus.

## What it Means to Fall from Grace

Galatians 5:4 (NKJV)
You have become estranged from Christ, you who attempt to be justified by law; you have fallen from grace.

When someone sins, oftentimes people say they fell from grace using the above Scripture as a reference. However, that is not what this verse means at all. Falling from grace has nothing to do with committing individual acts of sin.

Paul was dealing with people who had walked in God's grace, but were now attempting to be right with God by keeping the law. They were trying to earn God's acceptance by their performance. Taken in its context, to fall from grace means to stop living by grace and go back to trying to keep the law. It is when you stop living by God's unmerited favor and attempt to live by your own self-effort. It is performance-based living.

It is not difficult to live by the law; it is impossible! God wants us to live by His grace, which is His unmerited favor on our lives. Walking in grace is effortless living. It is being led by the Spirit. It is Spirit directed effort.

**Benefits of the New Covenant**

Psalm 103:1–5 (NKJV)
1 Bless the Lord, O my soul; And all that is within me, bless His holy name!
2 Bless the Lord, O my soul, And forget not all His benefits:
3 Who forgives all your iniquities, Who heals all your diseases,
4 Who redeems your life from destruction, Who crowns you with lovingkindness and tender mercies,
5 Who satisfies your mouth with good things, So that your youth is renewed like the eagle's.

The Lord loves you and wants you to be blessed. There are tons of blessings that belong to you in the new covenant. The psalmist tells us not to forget *all* His benefits. All things are yours because you are in Christ Jesus. Look at the benefits listed in this passage. The Lord forgives all of our iniquities. Some people think that the only thing that happened on the cross was that our sins were forgiven. But that is not all. There are other benefits. The Lord heals all our diseases, redeems our lives from destruction, crowns us with lovingkindness and tender mercies, and satisfies our mouths with good things, so that our youth is renewed like the eagle's. On the cross, Jesus took care of everything we need to succeed in life. Calvary covered it all. Constantly remind yourself of all the benefits that belong to you.

# CHAPTER FIVE

## *The Ministry of Reconciliation*

2 Corinthians 5:18–19 (NKJV)

18 Now all things are of God, who has reconciled us to Himself through Jesus Christ, and has given us the ministry of reconciliation,

19 that is, that God was in Christ reconciling the world to Himself, not imputing their trespasses to them, and has committed to us the word of reconciliation.

God was in Christ reconciling the world to Himself and not imputing their trespasses to them. The word *impute* is an accounting term. It means to charge to one's account. Jesus did not go around holding people's sins against them. He went about doing good and demonstrating God's goodness. He showed the world unconditional love. He told them they were forgiven. He did not tell people to stop sinning before He healed them.

It is important to remember that Jesus was the will of God in action. He never did anything that He did not see the Father do. This shows us that it is God's will for us to show unconditional love. Our job is not to point out people's sins; but rather to tell them they are forgiven.

## The Goodness of God

Romans 2:4 (NKJV)
4 Or do you despise the riches of His goodness, forbearance, and longsuffering, not knowing that the goodness of God leads you to repentance?

You can scare people into receiving salvation by talking about the fires and torments of hell, but that does not mean they want a relationship with God. They can pray the sinners' prayer and be born again. That is awesome. But that does not mean they will trust in Jesus and depend on Him as Lord of their lives. Many people pray the prayer as "fire" insurance and do not intend to have a relationship with Jesus.

God's method of getting people saved is to let them know how good He is. It is the goodness of God that leads people to repentance. People will want to follow Jesus when we let them know how good God is. We do not have to make the gospel attractive; it is already attractive. That is why it is called good news because you do not have to do anything to earn salvation. It is a gift. You do not work for it or deserve it; you simply receive it. The gospel is not a list of do's and don'ts. We just need to show people what the gospel really is. The good news is that all of the world's sins have been forgiven.

We have been given the same ministry as Jesus – the ministry of reconciliation. One definition of reconciling is to change a person from enmity to friendship. Under the old covenant, God was hostile toward man because of man's sins. However, under the new covenant, Jesus became sin for us. He took our place and died on our behalf. Our sins that caused God to be angry under the old covenant have been removed. Because of what Jesus did, God is no longer angry with man. The message of the cross is God bringing us back to Himself through Jesus Christ.

We should be doing what Jesus did, giving people the gospel. Many people today are doing the opposite of what Jesus did. They are going around pointing out people's sins. Our job is to tell people their sins are forgiven. All the world's sins have been charged to Jesus on the cross. He took our place. He was punished for our sins. And whom the Son sets free is free indeed.

We are forgiven and this is the message we are to proclaim to the world. They do not have to stop doing anything. All they have to do is receive what Jesus did for them by making Him the Lord of their lives.

**Nobody is Too Bad To Save**

Romans 10:13 (NKJV)
13 For *"whoever calls* on the name of the Lord shall be saved."

A man asked me a question after church one Sunday. After he heard me teach about God's grace and the new covenant, he wanted to know what would happen to a serial killer who accepts Jesus into his life. Would he be saved?

Think about it. Much of the Bible was written by murderers who received the grace of God - Moses, David, and Paul.

God does not see as man sees. His love for humanity is greater than we can imagine. God does not think like man. Nothing can compare to the love of God; nothing can match it.

Even people who think they have not been a bad person need a savior. We are not sinners because of what we do; we are sinners because of how we were born. We inherited the sin nature from Adam; therefore, everyone needs a savior.

So yes, God's love and mercy is available to us all, even the serial killer or others who have committed heinous crimes. All they have to do is believe and receive the gift of salvation.

# CHAPTER SIX

## *God's Love*

Jesus is the best example of how to show people love and acceptance. The people who were most upset with Him were religious people. The Bible says the common people heard Him gladly (Mark 12:37). He was constantly demonstrating the grace of God and showing people unconditional love.

The religious leaders of Jesus' day were shocked when Jesus spent time with sinners. However, Jesus told them, "Those who are well don't need a physician, but those who are sick (Matthew 9:12)."

For example, in John 8:1-11, there is a story about a time when some law teachers brought in a woman who was caught in adultery. They dragged her into the street and told Jesus that the law said she ought to be stoned and they asked Jesus' opinion. Jesus told them, "He who is without sin throw the first stone." They all started walking away. Jesus asked the woman, "Where are your accusers? Has no one condemned you?" She said, "No, Lord." And Jesus said, "Neither do I. Go your way and sin no more." Jesus refused to condemn the woman and that gave her the power to stop sinning.

In Luke 19:1-10, there was a man named Zacchaeus who wanted to see Jesus, but he was too short to see over the crowd. So, he ran ahead to where Jesus was going to be and climbed a tree to get a look at Him. Jesus saw him and told him to come down because He was going to be a guest at his home. Zacchaeus was so excited. Zacchaeus was a top agent for the IRS (who was not very well-liked in that day). He was also a wealthy man. Jesus showed love and acceptance to a man who was rarely shown love and acceptance. The religious leaders complained that Jesus went to be the guest of a sinner.

Look at this man's response to the goodness and love of God. He said, "I'm giving half of my wealth to the poor and if I cheated people on their taxes, I will pay back four times the amount." Jesus did not ask him to do that. That was his response to God's goodness.

Jesus said He came to seek and save the lost. Jesus is our example of how we should treat people. He was never hard on sinners. He was hard on religious people because they were mean and did not have people's best interest at heart. Jesus operated out of a motive of love because He is just like His Father. If you want to know what God is like, look at Jesus. Jesus only did what He saw the Father do. Jesus said, "He who has seen me has seen the Father (John 14:9)."

Jesus constantly spent time with people who the religious folks thought He should not. Jesus always showed mercy and compassion for those who were hurting. In John 4, Jesus was sitting by Jacob's well and a Samaritan woman came to the well to draw water. Jesus asked her for a drink. The woman was surprised that Jesus asked her for a drink because Jesus was a Jew and Jews did not associate with Samaritans.

The woman was also blown away because Jesus read her mail. He told her that she had five husbands and the man she was living with was not her husband. So, she was not a moral woman. Jesus was spending time with the kind of people that the religious crowd looked down on. This convinced her that Jesus was a prophet.

It is very interesting that many Christians today are reporting bad news and spreading a message that God is angry with people because of their lifestyles. The truth is that God is not angry with anyone today. He is a God of love. He not only has love, He is love (1 John 4:8). Jesus showed us exactly how we should treat people; yet, there are so many Christians going around yelling and shaking their Bibles at people to get them to repent. That is not God's way.

Jesus did not act independently of the Father. He only did what He saw the Father do. If you want to know what the Father is like, look at Jesus (John 5:19). Jesus was God manifested in the flesh

(1 Timothy 3:16). Read the gospels - Matthew, Mark, Luke, and John - to see God in action.

The Father loves you as much as He loves Jesus (John 14:23). Meditate on this truth. When you get a revelation of this truth, it will change your life forever. I used to make my love for God the main thing. Of course, that is important. But our focus should not be on our love for God. Our focus should be on His love for us (1 John 4:19). When we receive the love of God, we will be able to love ourselves and others.

The love of God is not a light truth. It is a fundamental truth, but it is a deep truth. The love of God is so deep that we will never be able to fully understand it. If you think you know everything you need to know about the love of God, think again.

Ephesians 3:19 (NLT)
19 May you experience the love of Christ, though it is too great to understand fully. Then you will be made complete with all the fullness of life and power that comes from God.

Because God loves you, He cares about and for you (1 Peter 5:7). God cares so much that every little thing that matters to you matters to Him. Jesus came to reveal the Father to us. Before Jesus came, no one referred to God as Father. The religious leaders thought it was blasphemous and were very upset when Jesus called God His Father. It is certainly right to call God by

His various biblical names, like El Shaddai, and Jehovah - Nissi, etc., but our default mode should be "Father." Jesus introduced the Father to us. Father is an intimate term. Abba means "Daddy" or "Papa." God Almighty is our Daddy.

Galatians 4:6 (NLT)
6 And because we are his children, God has sent the Spirit of his Son into our hearts, prompting us to call out, "Abba, Father."

It is interesting that the Holy Spirit saw fit to leave the word Abba untranslated in this verse and in Romans 8:15.

John 17:23 (NKJV)
23 I in them, and You in Me; that they may be made perfect in one, and that the world may know that You have sent Me, and **have loved them as You have loved Me**.

1 John 4:16 (NKJV)
16 And we have known and believed the love that God has for us. God is love, and he who abides in love abides in God, and God in him.

Believe in the love that God has for you.

Jesus prayed in John 17 that the world would come to know or realize that the Father loves us as much as He loved Him! Wow! The Father loves me as much as He loves Jesus. That is a powerful revelation contained in this prayer of Jesus! Do not take it lightly. When you understand that the Father loves you as much as He loves Jesus, you will understand that He will do anything for you. You will understand that He will give you the desires of your heart.

Romans 8:32 (NKJV)
32 He who did not spare His own Son, but delivered Him up for us all, how shall He not with Him also freely give us all things?

God loves you so much that He sent His only Son to die for you on the cross.

Once you realize God loves you, everything changes. Your self-esteem and faith will go through the roof. You will believe that your heavenly Father would do anything for you. That is why you can receive your healing and prosperity because His love provided them through Jesus. How much does He love you? Let me say it again. He loves you just as much as He loves Jesus!

Do you doubt the love that God has for Jesus? Of course not. Then, never doubt the love God has for you. Receive His love, reach out, and receive whatever you need or desire from Him.

## You Are Valuable

Ephesians 2:10 (NLT)
10 For we are God's masterpiece. He has created us anew in
Christ Jesus, so we can do the good things he planned for us long
ago.

You are God's masterpiece. You are God's handiwork. You are
unique. You are wonderfully put together by the God who created
the heavens and the earth (Psalm 139:14).

Consider a sculpture by Michelangelo, a painting by Rembrandt,
a violin by Stradivarius, or a play by Shakespeare. They are
valuable for two reasons:

1. They are few in number.
2. Their creators were masters.

For the same two reasons, you are the most valuable person on
the face of the earth. Almighty God is your creator and there is no
one on the face of the earth like you.[1]

The most important reason that you have great value is because
God sent His only son to die on the cross for you. He did that out
of His great love for you. That makes you extremely valuable and

---

[1] From Og Mandino's Memorandum from God (with adaptations)

special. You are God's beloved. God holds you in high esteem. You are the apple of His eye.

We need to remind ourselves constantly who we are in Christ Jesus. Why is this important? Because we are constantly faced with opportunities to look at either our circumstances or at what God says is already done. We are constantly facing things that come to us to knock us off our stand on the Word of God.

Hebrews 3:13 (Mirror)
13 Instead, remind one another daily of your true identity; make today count! Do not allow callousness of heart to cheat any of you for even a single day out of your allotted portion.

When faced with the choice of either looking at what is going on around us or looking at the Word, it is important for us to know God's opinion of us; how very important we are to Him. We need to know who we are in Christ.

You will be tempted almost every day to take your eyes off the Word. The devil is the accuser of the believer (Revelation 12:10). He often brings accusations against us. Sometimes they are accusations such as, you should be a better father, or you are a lousy mother, or you should be in better shape, or you should eat healthier, or you should be a nicer person, etc.

So, remind yourself daily of your true identity. Say, "I am righteous;" I am accepted in the beloved;" "I am approved;" "I am valuable;" "I am precious." "God holds me in high esteem."

Remind yourself of who you are to God and who He is to you. When you do that, you will have high self-esteem because you will know you are extremely valuable in His sight.

## What Does God See When He Looks at You?

1 John 4:17b (NKJV)
… as He is, so are we in this world.

This is a very important question. You need to know what God sees when He looks at you. Some people think that when God looks at them, he sees a failure or what they have done wrong. Others think God looks at their shortcomings but that is not what God sees when He looks at you.

When God looks at you, He sees Jesus! Wow! That is a powerful statement. And this does not apply just when you are doing good things. This is true even when you fall short because His love for you is not based on your goodness; it is based on His goodness.

As Jesus is so are you in this world. God has great love for you. There are no words in any language that can adequately describe our heavenly Father's love for us. Paul prayed that the Church of

Ephesus would be given the ability to comprehend what is the breadth, the length, the height, and the depth of His love.

When God looks at you, He does not see a worm or filthy rags. He sees you as the righteousness of God in Christ Jesus. He sees you righteous because He made you righteous. The Father loves you as much as He loves Jesus (John 17:23). And you know the Father loves Jesus! There is nothing God would not do for Jesus, so that means, there is nothing He would not do for you. Because God did not hold back His only Son, but offered Him up for us all, He will certainly freely give us all things (Romans 8:32).

See yourself today the way God sees you. God sees you "in Christ." He sees you as righteous and beloved.

## God Cares About the Small Stuff

Luke 12:7 (NCV)
7 But God even knows how many hairs you have on your head. Don't be afraid. You are worth much more than many sparrows.

Sparrows were very common in Israel at that time. They were inexpensive. Jesus said in Matthew 10:29 that you can get two sparrows for one copper coin. He said in Luke 12:6 that you can get five for two. If you do the math, you see that for two coins you get an extra sparrow thrown in! In other words, they do not cost very much. And Jesus said you are of more value than many sparrows.

Our heavenly Father even knows how many hairs you have on your head. That is not in the Bible to take up space. It is there to show you how valuable you are to God and how He cares about even the smallest details of your life.

God cares about the small things as well as the big things in your life. If it concerns you, you can talk to God about it no matter how small it is. You can talk to Him about a pimple on your face. Here is a powerful, but simple truth – your heavenly Father cares about you! God's love for you is personal. If it is important to you, it is important to Him. What you care about matters to Him. Why? Because He loves you and you matter to Him. You can go to God about anything.

When you know someone is busy, you could have a tendency not to want to bother talking to him or her about what you consider to be small stuff. But, God is not a man. He has time for you as if you were the only person in the world.

Your heavenly Father holds you in high esteem. You are extremely valuable in His eyes. So, do not hesitate to talk to Him about anything. If someone is giving you trouble on the job, do not think this is too small to take it to the Lord. You can talk with Him about a desire to go on a vacation with your family.

God is not only concerned about what you are dealing with, He is also able to provide you with the solution. You may have friends who will listen to you and try to console you, but they do not have the ability to do anything to solve your problem. However, your heavenly Father will not only listen, He is also able and willing to provide you with the help you need. He can handle your situation without breaking a sweat.

**Forgiveness Made Simple**

Colossians 3:13 (NKJV)
13 bearing with one another, and forgiving one another if anyone has a complaint against another; even as Christ forgave you, so you also must do.

God's Word makes forgiveness simple, but religion makes it complicated. Have you ever heard that you have to forgive and forget? The devil tries to add things to the Scriptures to put a burden on you such as, "If you did not forget, you really did not forgive." He tries to complicate what God made simple so he can place guilt on you.

You can forgive without forgetting. The Bible says Joseph remembered what his brothers did to him, but he did not hold it against them. His brothers had thrown him into a pit and left him there. But he did not harbor any anger or bitterness toward them (Genesis 50:15-21).

The Bible says forgive. Period. It does not add that we have to forget. When you forgive from your heart, do it by faith and eventually any anger or bitterness will go away. Whenever you feel any of that stuff trying to rise up in you, resist it because it is coming from the enemy. When you are resisting anything that comes from the devil, you are resisting him (James 4:7). And when you resist these negative emotions, they will flee from you.

God made forgiveness simple. He forgave us (unconditionally) - we forgive others (unconditionally). We forgive because He first forgave us and put His love in our heart so we can pass it on.

# CHAPTER SEVEN

## *You Are a Success*

Genesis 39:2 (NKJV)

2 The Lord was with Joseph, and he was a successful man; and he was in the house of his master the Egyptian.

Joseph was eventually promoted to second in command in Egypt, but he did not start there. He was bought from the slave market and became a slave in Potiphar's house. Yet, while he was a slave, God called Joseph a successful man. It is easy to look at others and say, "God can bless them because they are businessmen, doctors, or attorneys, but I am a custodian or a secretary. How can God bless me?"

I have good news for you today. It is not your job that determines your success. Do not think success is about achieving a particular destination in life such as making six figures or becoming a millionaire. No, no! You are already prosperous and successful because Jesus lives in you. God sees you as a success right now, and you need to see yourself the way God sees you. Say it aloud right now, "I am a successful person because Jesus lives in me."

## Don't Define Yourself by What You Do

2 Corinthians 5:17 (ESV)

17 Therefore, if anyone is in Christ, he is a new creation. The old has passed away; behold, the new has come.

Have you ever had someone approach you and ask you what you do? Many people today define themselves by what they do. As a believer in Christ, you are not what you do. You are who God says you are and that is how you define yourself. God says that you are "In Christ Jesus." There are over 100 "In Christ" scriptures in the New Testament. It is important to God that we know who we are.

God sees you in Christ. When God looks at you, He sees Jesus. As Jesus is so are you in this world (1 John 4:17). When you see yourself in Christ, you are seeing yourself the way God sees you.

How is Jesus doing? Is He struggling? No way! He is blessed and highly favored. Then, so are you in this world! You can be healed, prosper, and experience the blessings and favor of God, not because of what you do but because of who you are in Christ!

When you put your bank card in an ATM machine, it will ask you for a pin code. The pin code will give you access to your account. In the New Testament, we have been given exceedingly great and precious promises. And the pin code we use to access those promises is "In Christ." Our identity is in Him! See yourself in Christ Jesus.

## Prosperity and Good Success

3 John 2 (NKJV)
2 Beloved, I pray that you may prosper in all things and be in health, just as your soul prospers.

Since God wants us to prosper in all things, prosperity cannot be just one thing. When some people think of prosperity, they think only of money. Prosperity is spiritual, mental, physical, financial and social. Spiritual prosperity is being born again. Mental prosperity is having your mind renewed with God's Word. Physical prosperity is divine health. Financial prosperity is having plenty of money. Social prosperity is having good relationships with people.

Joshua 1:8 (NKJV)
8 This Book of the Law shall not depart from your mouth, but you shall meditate in it day and night, that you may observe to do according to all that is written in it. For then, you will make your way prosperous, and then you will have good success.

God wants us to have good success. Notice this verse does not just say success; it says good success. You can have success in life that is not good success. For example, when you have a million dollars in the bank, but your wife and kids will not talk to you, that is bad success. When you are healthy, but you are not born again, that is bad success.

Prosperity and good success are when you are born again, your mind is renewed with God's Word, you are healthy, you have good relationships with people, and you have more than enough financially.

# CHAPTER EIGHT

## *Relationship and Fellowship*

Hebrews 4:16 (NKJV)
Let us therefore come boldly to the throne of grace, that we may obtain mercy and find grace to help in time of need.

I want to expose a trick the devil uses to keep people from fellowshipping with God. Some people think that when they sin or make a mistake, they still have a relationship with God, but their sin caused them to be out of fellowship with God. However, that is not true.

When you were born again, you became one spirit with the Lord (1 Corinthians 6.17). You are joined with Him and nothing can separate you from His love. You cannot be out of fellowship.

The reason this is so important is because some people think that when they mess up, they cannot ask for His help. They think He has turned His back on them, but that is not the case. Even when you walk through the valley of the shadow of death, He is right there with you to pick up the pieces and lead you out. He wants you to come boldly to the throne of grace and receive His mercy. So, when you fall, do not run away from God; run to Him. He is right there with you and will never leave you or forsake you (Hebrews 13:5).

## Relationship Status: Righteous

On Facebook, some people describe their relationship status as complicated. Unfortunately, that describes the relationship status that many believers have with God today.

God does not want our relationship with Him to be complicated. That is what religion does. It makes relationship with God complicated. Religion attempts to get people to relate to God by keeping rules. But God wants our relationship with Him to be simple.

A relationship with God was complicated in the old covenant under the law. God's people had to keep many rules to be right with Him. In the new covenant under grace, Jesus made us right with God all by Himself. He made things simple for us. Instead of following a list of rules, we simply believe in the finished work of Jesus on the cross. Easy!

What is our relationship status with God? Righteous. That means we are right with God. We were made righteous based on what Jesus did. God wants to have fellowship with us.

Our heavenly Father wants our fellowship with Him to be free-flowing and smooth. He wants to walk and talk with us and to help us navigate through life. He wants to help us through difficult situations and to lead us beside the still waters. He wants us to talk to Him when we have a problem so He can lead us out of it. When we pray, we do not have to use religious jargon like thee's and thou's. We can just tell God what is on our hearts in our own communication style, slang and all! It is simple, not complicated.

Enjoy your relationship with God. You are the righteousness of God in Christ Jesus.

# CHAPTER NINE

## *Reigning in Life*

Romans 5:17 (AMP)
"For if because of one man's trespass (lapse, offense) death reigned through that one, much more surely will those who receive [God's] overflowing grace (unmerited favor) and the free gift of righteousness [putting them into right standing with Himself] reign as kings in life through the one Man Jesus Christ (the Messiah, the Anointed One)."

Genesis 1:26 (NLT)
"Then God said, "Let us make human beings in our image, to be like us. They will reign over the fish in the sea, the birds in the sky, the livestock, all the wild animals on the earth, and the small animals that scurry along the ground.""

2 Corinthians 2:14 (NKJV)
"Now thanks be to God who always leads us in triumph in Christ, and through us diffuses the fragrance of His knowledge in every place."

God wants you to win in life. He always leads us in triumph. How does He do it? He does it in Christ. God sees us in Christ. Christ is always a winner, so we are always winners. As He is, so are we in this world (1 John 4:17).

Ephesians 2:10 (AMP)

10 For we are God's [own] handiwork (His workmanship), recreated in Christ Jesus, [born anew] that we may do those good works which God predestined (planned beforehand) for us [taking paths which He prepared ahead of time], that we should walk in them [living the good life which He prearranged and made ready for us to live].

Jeremiah 1:5 (NCV)

5 "Before I made you in your mother's womb, I chose you....

Jeremiah 1:5 (AMP)

5 Before I formed you in the womb I knew [and] approved of you.....

You were created to have dominion! Start reigning. See yourself as a winner. You are already a success because Jesus lives in you.

You were not put on this earth to live an average or mundane life. You were put on this earth to have authority and dominion. Before you were formed in the womb, God chose and approved you. You were destined for success before the foundation of the world. Before you were born, God prearranged for you to live the good life. Your days were fashioned for you before you had days (Psalm 139:16). God has a wonderful plan for your life!

Hebrews 5:13 (NKJV)

13 For everyone who partakes only of milk is unskilled in the word of righteousness, for he is a babe.

A spiritual baby is someone who does not understand righteousness. Being a mature Christian is not about how much knowledge you can accumulate. Because someone is good at Bible trivia games and can answer a ton of Bible facts does not mean that person is reigning in life. It does not mean that person knows what it means to be righteous.

If someone preaches about how to become more righteous, that individual does not understand righteousness. We always need to evaluate whether things we hear are from the Word of God, even when it comes from ministers. Then, we will not be fooled and miss out on the abundant life that God has for us.

Let us look at what righteousness is not and what it is.

What righteousness is not:

1. A goal to be achieved.
2. Something to be earned.
3. Something you grow in.

What righteousness is:

1. A gift to be received by faith.
2. A position that you are placed in the moment you accept Christ.
3. A state of being.

You are as righteous as you are ever going to be. You will never be more righteous in heaven than you are right now. You are as righteous as Jesus is because you are in Him. This is the way God sees you; so, see yourself that way.

## Righteous by Nature

Romans 5:18–19 (ESV)
18 Therefore, as one trespass led to condemnation for all men, so one act of righteousness leads to justification and life for all men. 19 For as by the one man's disobedience the many were made sinners, so by the one man's obedience the many will be made righteous.

Just as nothing we did made us sinners (we were sinners because of Adam), nothing we do can make us righteous (we are righteous because of Jesus). Righteousness is a gift. All we have to do is receive it. We did not deserve to be made sinners. Adam put us in that predicament. Even so, we did not deserve to be made righteous. Jesus made us righteous. We are righteous because of what Jesus did for us.

Before you are born again, you are a sinner by nature. No good works that you do can change your sin nature. Your goodness cannot change your badness. On the other hand, when you become born again, you are righteous by nature. No bad works that you do can change your righteous nature. Your badness cannot change your goodness.

One act made us sinners and one act made us righteous. You are the righteousness of God in Christ Jesus.

When you receive God's grace and the gift of righteousness, you will reign in life as a king. When you reign, lack cannot reign, sickness cannot reign, depression cannot reign, addictions cannot reign. God wants you to reign in your finances, health, business, relationships and family life.

**Benefits of Walking in Righteousness**

Psalm 84:11 (NKJV)
"For the Lord God is a sun and shield; The Lord will give grace and glory; No good thing will He withhold from those who walk uprightly."

Galatians 2:14 (KJV)
"But when I saw that they walked not uprightly according to the truth of the gospel, …

God showed Peter through a vision and personal experience that salvation was for the Gentiles as well as the Jews. However, Paul walked in a higher revelation of grace than Peter.

In Galatians 2, Peter was eating and fellowshipping with the Gentiles. But when certain Jews came, he separated himself from them. His hypocrisy even influenced Barnabas to do the same. Paul confronted Peter and told him he was not walking uprightly according to the truth of the gospel.

Galatians 2:16, NKJV
"Knowing that a man is not justified by the works of the law but by faith in Jesus Christ, even we have believed in Christ Jesus, that we might be justified by faith in Christ and not by the works of the law; for by the works of the law no flesh shall be justified."

The law came through Moses, but grace and truth came by Jesus Christ. Grace is the truth of the gospel (John 1:17).
To walk uprightly means to walk in your righteousness that you receive as a grace gift.

The conclusion of Psalm 84:11 is that no good thing will God withhold from you when you walk in your righteousness! God will surely give you all things (Romans 8:32)!

Confess three times: "I am the righteousness of God in Christ Jesus."

# CHAPTER TEN
## *The Blessings Belong to Us*

Deuteronomy 28:1–2 (NKJV)

1 "Now it shall come to pass, if you diligently obey the voice of the Lord your God, to observe carefully all His commandments which I command you today, that the Lord your God will set you high above all nations of the earth.

2 And all these blessings shall come upon you and overtake you, because you obey the voice of the Lord your God:

Deuteronomy 28 summarizes the blessings and curses of the law. All those blessings will come upon you and overtake you if you diligently obey God's voice and observe carefully *all* of God's commandments. The problem is that none of us can keep all God's commandments. That is why we needed a savior. The purpose of the law was so that the world would have the knowledge of sin (Romans 3:20) and recognize their need for a savior. The law was our tutor to bring us to Christ (James 2:24).

James 2:10 (NLT)

10 For the person who keeps all of the laws except one is as guilty as a person who has broken all of God's laws.

It is not good enough to keep some of God's laws. Under the old covenant, it was not good enough to keep some of the law. Getting 99% of the law right equals failure. There is no A, B, C, and D with God. Neither does God grade on a curve. It is either A+ or F. James says that whoever keeps the entire law but misses it in one point is guilty of all.

The good news is that Jesus is the fulfillment of the law.

Matthew 5:17 (AMP)
17 Do not think that I have come to do away with or undo the Law or the Prophets; I have come not to do away with or undo but to complete and fulfill them.

Jesus is the only one who kept the law perfectly. He hearkened diligently to the voice of the Lord and did everything that was pleasing in God's sight.

Galatians 3:13–14 (NKJV)
13 Christ has redeemed us from the curse of the law, having become a curse for us (for it is written, "Cursed is everyone who hangs on a tree"),
14 that the blessing of Abraham might come upon the Gentiles in Christ Jesus, that we might receive the promise of the Spirit through faith.

Not only did Jesus keep the law perfectly, but He also redeemed us from the law's curse so we could have the blessings of Abraham. Jesus took our place on the cross and became a curse for us. Because He kept all of the commandments perfectly and became a curse for us, the blessings of Abraham are ours.

When we interpret the Old Testament in light of the finished work, we understand that the blessings in Deuteronomy apply to us today because Christ kept the law perfectly and redeemed us from the curse so that the blessings of Abraham would come on us.

All we have to do to receive these blessings is to receive by faith what Jesus did for us on the cross. These blessings include being blessed in the city and in the country, being blessed coming in and going out, and prospering in whatever we do. Praise God!

**All of God's Promises Are Yes In Christ**

2 Corinthians 1:20 (NKJV)
For all the promises of God in Him are Yes, and in Him Amen, to the glory of God through us.

Do you desire something from God today? We have all had someone who said they were going to do something and then did not do it. Paul was letting us know that God is not like that. God is not yes and no. He does not say He is going to do something and then not do it. God's Word said, "...by His stripes, you were healed," so He is not going to say no when you come to Him for healing. The answer is already yes.

In the Old Testament, the promises of God were conditional; they were based on keeping the Commandments.

Deuteronomy 28:1–2 (NKJV)
1 "Now it shall come to pass, if you diligently obey the voice of the Lord your God, to observe carefully all His commandments which I command you today, that the Lord your God will set you high above all nations of the earth. 2 And all these blessings shall come upon you and overtake you, because you obey the voice of the Lord your God:

The problem with the old covenant was that nobody could keep the law. The good news is that, what we could not do, God did by sending Jesus. He took our place and fulfilled the law on our behalf. He kept all the commandments, lived a sinless life, conquered Satan in every area, and died in our place.

That is why all of God's promises in Christ are yes and amen.

Here is the bottom line: Jesus qualified us to receive all the promises of God.

We see in Jesus' earthly ministry that He never refused to heal anyone who came to Him for healing. He never told anyone that it was God's will to leave him or her sick. Jesus was the will of God in action. He only did what He saw His Father do. Jesus said *yes* to everyone who came to Him for healing or deliverance. This shows us that it is God's will to heal *all*.

Jesus is the same yesterday, today, and forever (Hebrews 13:8). He did not turn anyone away then, and He will not turn anyone away now. This is not only true concerning healing but it is also true for all of God's promises. You can receive anything you need from God today, whether it is healing, a financial breakthrough, or whatever.

When you ask God for a promise in His Word, He will never tell you no or maybe. His answer to you is yes and amen. His promises are true. Believe them. They belong to you as His beloved child. Whenever you hear a promise from God, be assured that the answer is - yes! Receive your blessing from God today.

One more thing, beware of the devil who likes to point you to yourself and tell you that you do not deserve to get what you want because of something you have done. He tries to make you self-conscious. Do not put up with Satan's lies. Point him to Jesus. It is not about your obedience; it is about Jesus' obedience. The promises are not yes in you, but yes *in Him*. He cannot mess with that.

# CHAPTER ELEVEN

## *God Will Open and Close Doors for You*

### Open Doors

Revelation 3:7 (NKJV)
"And to the angel of the church in Philadelphia write, 'These things says He who is holy, He who is true, "He who has the key of David, He who opens and no one shuts, and shuts and no one opens"

Because of Gods unmerited favor on your life, He will open doors for you. No man has the ability to shut the doors that God opens in your life. Do not be afraid when someone is trying to assassinate your character or do you wrong. No weapon formed against you shall prosper (Isaiah 54:17). Trust God to take care of you. He always has your back.

Hebrews 13:6 (NKJV)
6 So we may boldly say: "The Lord is my helper; I will not fear. What can man do to me?"

He will never leave you or forsake you; so do not fear whatever someone is trying do to you. No matter what plan people devise against you, God says that you are more than a conqueror and God's Word will always prevail.

## Closed Doors

I think sometimes we under-praise God. What I mean is that it is easy to thank God for the doors He opens in our lives. But what about the doors He closes. When God closes a door, there is a reason. If the Lord allowed you to walk through that door, something could have happened that would have been detrimental to you and your family. So, He shuts that door.

God sees things we cannot. There are times in our lives that He keeps us from problems we will never know about. We need to thank God for those things. We should praise God for the things He delivers us from, but let us also thank God for the bad situations in life we will never experience because He watches over us and works everything together for our good. If He would allow us to see all the trouble He has kept us from, we would dance and shout!

For example, He may have you stop at the grocery store on your way to work to keep you from a tragic accident that you would have been involved in if you had not stopped at the store. You may not even hear about that accident that He had you avoid. A company may be very close to offering you a job; then unexpectedly, you do not get the offer. You may wonder why. Sometimes, it is because God closed that door. He knew that in the end, that job would not be good for you. Trust Him that when

He closes the door, He will also open doors for you. Look for the open door.

God is the master traffic controller in the believer's life. In addition to praising God for what He delivers us from, let us also thank Him for the unknown things He keeps us from.

# CHAPTER TWELVE

## *What About Sin?*

**What Do I Do When I Sin?**

Hebrews 4:16 (NCV)
16 Let us, then, feel very sure that we can come before God's throne where there is grace. There we can receive mercy and grace to help us when we need it.

When you sin, go to God and receive mercy and grace to help. Mercy is **not getting** what you **deserve**, and grace **is getting** what you **do not deserve**. One of the reasons people do not go to God when they sin is because they think He is mad at them. God will never stop loving you no matter what you do.

Jeremiah 31:3 (The Message)… God told them, "I've never quit loving you and never will. Expect love, love, and more love!

When Adam sinned in the Garden of Eden, he hid himself from God. God was seeking him out, but he was in hiding. Adam's sin did not change God's opinion of him; God did not stop loving him. Adam's sin distorted his view of God.

Many people today do the same thing. When they sin, they run away from God instead of running to Him. Whenever you fail, you should go to your heavenly Father to receive help for your failures understanding that He is not angry with you when you sin. God wants you to feel free to come to Him when you are hurting, stressed, in pain, or dealing with a difficult situation. Understanding this will help you see that you can go to God and receive His grace to help you when you do sin. Go to your Father and get help when you need it.

## Sin Is Not Your Master

When you are under grace, sin will not control you. You will walk in victory over it. The majority of God's people are not looking to get into sin; they are looking for a way out. I am telling you grace is the way out. Receive God's abundance of grace and His gift of righteousness and you will reign over sin.

Romans 6:14 (NCV)
14 Sin will not be your master, because you are not under law but under God's grace.

God's grace does not encourage you to sin; it gives you dominion over sin.

## Do Not Focus on Sin

1 Corinthians 15:56 (NKJV)
56 The sting of death is sin, and the strength of sin is the law.

Focusing on "thou shalt not" (the law) will strengthen sin and cause it to increase.

One thing to do about sin is to not think about it. Instead, think about Jesus, the Word of God. Think about how much God loves you and how well pleased He is with you. You are accepted in the beloved. In other words, focus on who you are in Christ. I encourage you to meditate on the "In Christ" scriptures at the back of this book.

# CHAPTER THIRTEEN

## *God is Not Judging You*

Many ministers, from the pulpit, are preaching that God is judging America through the bad things that have happened such as terrorist attacks or natural disasters. Let us look at what God's Word says.

John 3:17 (AMP)
17 For God did not send the Son into the world in order to judge (to reject, to condemn, to pass sentence on) the world, but that the world might find salvation and be made safe and sound through Him.

Luke 2:14 (NLT)
14 "Glory to God in highest heaven, and peace on earth to those with whom God is pleased."

God is not judging America or any other place. He did not come to judge or condemn the world. He came to save the world. Jesus came to bring peace on earth between God and man.

2 Peter 3:9 (NLT)
9 The Lord isn't really being slow about his promise, as some people think. No, he is being patient for your sake. He does not want anyone to be destroyed, but wants everyone to repent.

God is a God of love, mercy, and grace; therefore, He does not want anyone to be destroyed.

In the Old Testament, God did judge people because of their sins. Let us look at a couple of Old Testament examples.

1. Elijah Calling Down Fire From Heaven

2 Kings 1:9–12 (NLT)

9 Then he sent an army captain with fifty soldiers to arrest him. They found him sitting on top of a hill. The captain said to him, "Man of God, the king has commanded you to come down with us."

10 But Elijah replied to the captain, "If I am a man of God, let fire come down from heaven and destroy you and your fifty men!" Then fire fell from heaven and killed them all.

11 So the king sent another captain with fifty men. The captain said to him, "Man of God, the king demands that you come down at once."

12 Elijah replied, "If I am a man of God, let fire come down from heaven and destroy you and your fifty men!" And again the fire of God fell from heaven and killed them all.

King Ahaziah was a wicked king who was mad at Elijah. He sent a captain with a group of fifty men to capture him. Elijah called fire down from heaven and consumed them all. The king then sent another captain with a set of fifty men to bring Elijah back and the same thing happened to them.

Luke 9:51–56 (NKJV)
51 Now it came to pass, when the time had come for Him to be received up, that He steadfastly set His face to go to Jerusalem,
52 and sent messengers before His face. And as they went, they entered a village of the Samaritans, to prepare for Him.
53 But they did not receive Him, because His face was set for the journey to Jerusalem.
54 And when His disciples James and John saw this, they said, "Lord, do You want us to command fire to come down from heaven and consume them, just as Elijah did?"
55 But He turned and rebuked them, and said, "You do not know what manner of spirit you are of.
56 For the Son of Man did not come to destroy men's lives but to save them." And they went to another village.

Jesus' disciples went ahead of Him to prepare for Him. Because the people did not want to receive Jesus, James and John asked Jesus if He wanted them to call for fire from heaven to consume the people as Elijah had. They wanted to jack those cats up! Jesus explained to them that they did not have that kind of spirit. Jesus was showing them the way of the new covenant. Jesus told them He did not come to destroy men's lives but to save their lives.

2. Destruction of Sodom

The city of Sodom was exceedingly wicked. God sent angels there to destroy the city because of its great wickedness.

Genesis 18:32 (NLT)
32 Finally, Abraham said, "Lord, please don't be angry with me if I speak one more time. Suppose only ten are found there?" And the Lord replied, "Then I will not destroy it for the sake of the ten."

Abraham negotiated with God and asked Him if He would spare the city if there were just ten righteous people in it, and God told Abraham He would spare it for the sake of the ten.

Genesis 19:22 (NLT)
22 But hurry! Escape to it, for I can do nothing until you arrive there." (This explains why that village was known as Zoar, which means "little place.")

The angel instructed Lot to get his family out of there. Lot asked the angel if he could go to a small nearby village. The angel granted his request. The angel could not destroy the city until Lot left. Here we see that God would have spared the city even if only one righteous person were there. This is a demonstration of God's mercy even in the old covenant.

## God is Not Judging You Today Because of What Jesus Did for You on the Cross

It is important to understand that the stories of Elijah and Sodom occurred before the cross. Jesus in His great commission in Matthew 28:20 told the disciples to make other disciples and teach them to observe all the things He had commanded them. He wanted them to teach the new covenant and what He taught them here is a new covenant revelation. All of God's judgment for all our sins for all time fell on Jesus on the cross.

Even if God desired to judge America today, He could not do it because there is at least one righteous person living here!

John 3:16 (NKJV)
16 For God so loved the world that He gave His only begotten Son, that whoever believes in Him should not perish but have everlasting life.

God is no longer angry with man because of man's sins. He told James and John that this was not the kind of spirit they had, one of judgment. He did not come to destroy people's lives; that is what the devil does (John 10:10). Satan's job is to steal, kill, and destroy. Jesus came to save the world, not condemn it (John 3:17). The reason God cannot judge you for your sins today is because Jesus has already been judged for your sins. That is good news!

# CHAPTER FOURTEEN

## *The Holy Spirit*

### The Holy Spirit Does Not Convict the Believer of Sins

John 16:7–10 (NKJV)

7 Nevertheless I tell you the truth. It is to your advantage that I go away; for if I do not go away, the Helper will not come to you; but if I depart, I will send Him to you.

8 And when He has come, He will convict the world of sin, and of righteousness, and of judgment:

9 of sin, because they do not believe in Me;

10 of righteousness, because I go to My Father and you see Me no more;

This passage is not teaching us that the Holy Spirit is convicting believers of sins. The Holy Spirit will convict the world of sin. The world refers to people who do not believe in Jesus. Notice that the word *sin* is singular and not plural.

The English word *convict* means to declare someone *to be guilty*. Many believers think the word *convict* in this passage of scripture is a negative word. When some Christians talk about the convicting of the Holy Spirit, they describe it as Him being harsh and condemning. They give the idea that He will jump all over us when we mess up. One of the meanings of convict is convince. I believe this is a more accurate word for what the Holy Spirit does because it is consistent with His nature.

What is the Holy Spirit convincing the world of? Jesus said the Holy Spirit will convince the world of sin because they do not believe in Him. Rejecting Jesus is the only sin the Holy Spirit is convincing the world of. The Holy Spirit's work in unbelievers is to convince them that they need a savior. He does this through the preaching of the Word (1 Corinthians 1:21). When the Word of God is preached, the Holy Spirit goes to work to convince an individual to make Jesus Christ the Lord of his or her life.

The Holy Spirit will also convince believers of righteousness. The Holy Spirit's job is to convince us that we are the righteousness of God in Christ. The work of the Holy Spirit in believers' lives is to lead us and guide us, not to whip us into shape. This distorted view of the Holy Spirit comes from an inaccurate view of how God sees us.

The Holy Spirit will never do anything that the Father would not do. He will never beat you up because the Father would never beat you up. The Father would not make you feel guilty for your sins, so neither would the Holy Spirit. Some people say the Holy Spirit made them miserable because of something they did wrong. But, that is not the nature of the Holy Spirit.

The Holy Spirit is a gentleman. A gentleman will be gentle. The Holy Spirit does not have a harsh nature; He has a gentle one. Furthermore, you would not want to spend time with someone if all he did was point out your faults. The devil wants to get you to believe that the Holy Spirit points out your sins and shortcomings, so that you would not want to have a relationship with Him. But, the Holy Spirit wants to be in close fellowship with you.

John 16:7 (AMP)
7… I will send Him (the Holy Spirit) to you [to be in close fellowship with you].

The Holy Spirit does not condone sin and neither does God. Father God, Jesus and the Holy Spirit do not want you to feel bad about your sins. So, what does the Holy Spirit do when we sin? How does the Holy Spirit respond when we sin? He does what Jesus sent Him to do. He helps us. He will convince you that you are the righteousness of God in Christ. He will convince you of who you are. He will show you the way out.

I have a navigation system in my car. I can tell it where I want to go, and it will lead me there. If I make a wrong turn, it does not get angry with me. It will simply redirect me. It will tell me where to turn to get back on the right track. It never changes its tone. Regardless of the number of times that I do not follow the directions and make wrong turns, it continues giving me instructions to get me back on the right track.

This is what the Holy Spirit does for us. No matter how many times we miss it, He keeps guiding us and showing us the way back to where God wants us to be. He is not here to make our lives miserable. He is here to lead us into the abundant life that God has for us.

## The Holy Spirit Reveals God's Favor

1 Corinthians 2:9–10 (NKJV)
9 But as it is written: "Eye has not seen, nor ear heard, Nor have entered into the heart of man The things which God has prepared for those who love Him."
10 But God has revealed them to us through His Spirit. For the Spirit searches all things, yes, the deep things of God.

God has prepared some wonderful things for us and He wants us to know what they are. If you prepared something special for someone, would you not want that person to know what you prepared for him or her? Well, God is the same way.

Some people quote verse 9 but do not read the next verse. If you just look at that verse, it appears that we cannot know what God has prepared for us. Many ministers focus on the part that says eye has not seen, nor ear heard. But if you continue reading, you will discover that God has revealed the things He has prepared for us. And the way He chooses to reveal them is through the Spirit.

1 Corinthians 2:12 (AMP)

Now we have not received the spirit [that belongs to] the world, but the [Holy] Spirit Who is from God, [given to us] that we might realize and comprehend and appreciate the gifts [of divine favor and blessing so freely and lavishly] bestowed on us by God.

The Holy Spirit has been given to us to help us understand and appreciate the unmerited favor that God has freely and lavishly bestowed upon us. Our heavenly Father has lavish blessings that are already prepared for us. We do not work for them; we just receive them.

# CHAPTER FIFTEEN

## *Don't Quit*

Are you going through tough times and being tempted to give up? I want to encourage you with these three simple words, "Do not quit!"

Paul was facing persecution from the enemy. He pleaded with God three times to take it away.

2 Corinthians 12:7–9 (The Message)
… Satan's angel did his best to get me down; what he in fact did was push me to my knees..…
9 and then he told me, My grace is enough; it's all you need. My strength comes into its own in your weakness. Once I heard that, I was glad to let it happen. ….It was a case of Christ's strength moving in on my weakness.

Regardless of what you may be up against, let me give you a reason not to quit - God's grace is enough. His love will never fail you. God will never leave you for one second or give up on you (Hebrews 13:5). Not now, not ever.

So, hold your head up high knowing that in Christ Jesus you are more than a conqueror (Romans 8:37). You are a winner and a champion in Christ Jesus (1 Corinthians 15:57). Greater is He who is in you than He who is in the world (1 John 4:4). You are the disciple whom Jesus loves and He will care for you and provide for you (John 21:20; 1 Peter 5:7). He is right there with you carrying you through this battle. Trust Him and be sure of this; you are coming out on top. You are not alone. Be strong in the Lord and in the power of His might (Ephesians 6:10). Let His strength move in on your weakness. His unmerited favor on your life is on you now, and it is enough.

# In Christ Scriptures

Romans 1:5 Through Him we have received grace and apostleship for obedience to the faith among all nations for His name,

Romans 3:24 being justified freely by His grace through the redemption that is in Christ Jesus,

Romans 5:2 through whom also we have access by faith into this grace in which we stand, and rejoice in hope of the glory of God.

Romans 5:9 Much more then, having now been justified by His blood, we shall be saved from wrath through Him.

Romans 5:11 And not only that, but we also rejoice in God through our Lord Jesus Christ, through whom we have now received the reconciliation.

Romans 6:11 Likewise you also, reckon yourselves to be dead indeed to sin, but alive to God in Christ Jesus our Lord.

Romans 6:23 For the wages of sin is death, but the gift of God is eternal life in Christ Jesus our Lord.

Romans 8:1 There is therefore now no condemnation to those who are in Christ Jesus, who do not walk according to the flesh, but according to the Spirit.

Romans 8:2 For the law of the Spirit of life in Christ Jesus has made me free from the law of sin and death.

Romans 8:37 Yet in all these things we are more than conquerors through Him who loved us.

Romans 8:39 nor height nor depth, nor any other created thing, shall be able to separate us from the love of God which is in Christ Jesus our Lord.

Romans 9:1 I tell the truth in Christ, I am not lying, my conscience also bearing me witness in the Holy Spirit,

Romans 11:36 For of Him and through Him and to Him are all things, to whom be glory forever. Amen.

Romans 12:5 so we, being many, are one body in Christ, and individually members of one another.

Romans 15:17 Therefore I have reason to glory in Christ Jesus in the things which pertain to God.

Romans 16:3 Greet Priscilla and Aquila, my fellow workers in Christ Jesus,

Romans 16:7 Greet Andronicus and Junia, my countrymen and my fellow prisoners, who are of note among the apostles, who also were in Christ before me.

Romans 16:9 Greet Urbanus, our fellow worker in Christ, and Stachys, my beloved.

Romans 16:10 Greet Apelles, approved in Christ. Greet those who are of the household of Aristobulus.

1 Corinthians. 1:2 To the church of God which is at Corinth, to those who are sanctified in Christ Jesus, called to be saints, with all who in every place call on the name of Jesus Christ our Lord, both theirs and ours:

1 Corinthians 1:9 God is faithful, by whom you were called into the fellowship of His Son, Jesus Christ our Lord.

1 Corinthians 1:30 But of Him you are in Christ Jesus, who became for us wisdom from God—and righteousness and sanctification and redemption—

1 Corinthians 3:1 And I, brethren, could not speak to you as to spiritual people but as to carnal, as to babes in Christ.

1 Corinthians 4:10 We are fools for Christ's sake, but you are wise in Christ! We are weak, but you are strong! You are distinguished, but we are dishonored!

1 Corinthians 4:15 For though you might have ten thousand instructors in Christ, yet you do not have many fathers; for in Christ Jesus I have begotten you through the gospel.

1 Corinthians 4:17 For this reason I have sent Timothy to you, who is my beloved and faithful son in the Lord, who will remind you of my ways in Christ, as I teach everywhere in every church.

1 Corinthians 8:6 yet for us there is one God, the Father, of whom are all things, and we for Him; and one Lord Jesus Christ, through whom are all things, and through whom we live.

1 Corinthians 15:18 Then also those who have fallen asleep in Christ have perished.

1 Corinthians 15:19 If in this life only we have hope in Christ, we are of all men the most pitiable.

1 Corinthians 15:22 For as in Adam all die, even so in Christ all shall be made alive.

1 Corinthians 15:31 I affirm, by the boasting in you which I have in Christ Jesus our Lord, I die daily.

1 Corinthians 16:24 My love be with you all in Christ Jesus. Amen.

2 Corinthians 1:5 For as the sufferings of Christ abound in us, so our consolation also abounds through Christ.

2 Corinthians 1:10 who delivered us from so great a death, and does deliver us; in whom we trust that He will still deliver us,

2 Corinthians 1:19 For the Son of God, Jesus Christ, who was preached among you by us—by me, Silvanus, and Timothy—was not Yes and No, but in Him was Yes.

2 Corinthians 1:20 For all the promises of God in Him are Yes, and in Him Amen, to the glory of God through us.

2 Corinthians 1:21 Now He who establishes us with you in Christ and has anointed us is God,

2 Corinthians 2:14 Now thanks be to God who always leads us in triumph in Christ, and through us diffuses the fragrance of His knowledge in every place.

2 Corinthians 2:17 For we are not, as so many, peddling the word of God; but as of sincerity, but as from God, we speak in the sight of God in Christ.

2 Corinthians 3:4 And we have such trust through Christ toward God.

2 Corinthians 3:14 But their minds were blinded. For until this day the same veil remains unlifted in the reading of the Old Testament, because the veil is taken away in Christ.

2 Corinthians 5:17 Therefore, if anyone is in Christ, he is a new creation; old things have passed away; behold, all things have become new.

2 Corinthians 5:19 that is, that God was in Christ reconciling the world to Himself, not imputing their trespasses to them, and has committed to us the word of reconciliation.

2 Corinthians 5:21 For He made Him who knew no sin to be sin for us, that we might become the righteousness of God in Him.

2 Corinthians 11:3 But I fear, lest somehow, as the serpent deceived Eve by his craftiness, so your minds may be corrupted from the simplicity that is in Christ.

2 Corinthians 12:2 I know a man in Christ who fourteen years ago—whether in the body I do not know, or whether out of the body I do not know, God knows—such a one was caught up to the third heaven.

2 Corinthians 12:19 Again, do you think that we excuse ourselves to you? We speak before God in Christ. But we do all things, beloved, for your edification.

2 Corinthians 13:4 For though He was crucified in weakness, yet He lives by the power of God. For we also are weak in Him, but we shall live with Him by the power of God toward you.

Galatians 1:22 And I was unknown by face to the churches of Judea which were in Christ.

Galatians 2:4 And this occurred because of false brethren secretly brought in (who came in by stealth to spy out our liberty which we have in Christ Jesus, that they might bring us into bondage),

Galatians 3:14 that the blessing of Abraham might come upon the Gentiles in Christ Jesus, that we might receive the promise of the Spirit through faith.

Galatians 3:17 And this I say, that the law, which was four hundred and thirty years later, cannot annul the covenant that was confirmed before by God in Christ, that it should make the promise of no effect.

Galatians 3:26 For you are all sons of God through faith in Christ Jesus.

Galatians 3:28 There is neither Jew nor Greek, there is neither slave nor free, there is neither male nor female; for you are all one in Christ Jesus.

Galatians 4:7 Therefore you are no longer a slave but a son, and if a son, then an heir of God through Christ.

Galatians 5:6 For in Christ Jesus neither circumcision nor uncircumcision avails anything, but faith working through love.

Galatians 6:14 But God forbid that I should boast except in the cross of our Lord Jesus Christ, by whom the world has been crucified to me, and I to the world.

Galatians 6:15 For in Christ Jesus neither circumcision nor uncircumcision avails anything, but a new creation.

Ephesians 1:1 Paul, an apostle of Jesus Christ by the will of God, To the saints who are in Ephesus, and faithful in Christ Jesus:

Ephesians 1:3 Blessed be the God and Father of our Lord Jesus Christ, who has blessed us with every spiritual blessing in the heavenly places in Christ,

Ephesians 1:4 just as He chose us in Him before the foundation of the world, that we should be holy and without blame before Him in love,

Ephesians 1:7 In Him we have redemption through His blood, the forgiveness of sins, according to the riches of His grace

Ephesians 1:10 that in the dispensation of the fullness of the times He might gather together in one all things in Christ, both which are in heaven and which are on earth—in Him.

Ephesians 1:11 In Him also we have obtained an inheritance, being predestined according to the purpose of Him who works all things according to the counsel of His will,

Ephesians 1:12 that we who first trusted in Christ should be to the praise of His glory.

Ephesians 1:13 In Him you also trusted, after you heard the word of truth, the gospel of your salvation; in whom also, having believed, you were sealed with the Holy Spirit of promise,

Ephesians 1:20 which He worked in Christ when He raised Him from the dead and seated Him at His right hand in the heavenly places,

Ephesians 2:6 and raised us up together, and made us sit together in the heavenly places in Christ Jesus,

Ephesians 2:7 that in the ages to come He might show the exceeding riches of His grace in His kindness toward us in Christ Jesus.

Ephesians 2:10 For we are His workmanship, created in Christ Jesus for good works, which God prepared beforehand that we should walk in them.

Ephesians 2:13 But now in Christ Jesus you who once were far off have been brought near by the blood of Christ.

Ephesians 2:18 For through Him we both have access by one Spirit to the Father.

Ephesians 2:21 in whom the whole building, being fitted together, grows into a holy temple in the Lord,

Ephesians 2:22 in whom you also are being built together for a dwelling place of God in the Spirit.

Ephesians 3:6 that the Gentiles should be fellow heirs, of the same body, and partakers of His promise in Christ through the gospel,

Ephesians 3:11 according to the eternal purpose which He accomplished in Christ Jesus our Lord,

Ephesians 3:12 in whom we have boldness and access with confidence through faith in Him.

Ephesians 4:32 And be kind to one another, tenderhearted, forgiving one another, even as God in Christ forgave you.

Philippians 1:1 Paul and Timothy, bondservants of Jesus Christ, To all the saints in Christ Jesus who are in Philippi, with the bishops and deacons:

Philippians 1:13 so that it has become evident to the whole palace guard, and to all the rest, that my chains are in Christ;

Philippians 1:29 For to you it has been granted on behalf of Christ, not only to believe in Him, but also to suffer for His sake,

Philippians 2:1 Therefore if there is any consolation in Christ, if any comfort of love, if any fellowship of the Spirit, if any affection and mercy,

Philippians 2:5 Let this mind be in you which was also in Christ Jesus,

Philippians 3:3 For we are the circumcision, who worship God in the Spirit, rejoice in Christ Jesus, and have no confidence in the flesh,

Philippians 3:9 and be found in Him, not having my own righteousness, which is from the law, but that which is through faith in Christ, the righteousness which is from God by faith;

Philippians 3:14 I press toward the goal for the prize of the upward call of God in Christ Jesus.

Philippians 4:7 and the peace of God, which surpasses all understanding, will guard your hearts and minds through Christ Jesus.

Philippians 4:13 I can do all things through Christ who strengthens me.

Philippians 4:21 Greet every saint in Christ Jesus. The brethren who are with me greet you.

Colossians 1:2 To the saints and faithful brethren in Christ who are in Colosse: Grace to you and peace from God our Father and the Lord Jesus Christ.

Colossians 1:4 since we heard of your faith in Christ Jesus and of your love for all the saints;

Colossians 1:14 in whom we have redemption through His blood, the forgiveness of sins.

Colossians 1:16 For by Him all things were created that are in heaven and that are on earth, visible and invisible, whether thrones or dominions or principalities or powers. All things were created through Him and for Him.

Colossians 1:17 And He is before all things, and in Him all things consist.

Colossians 1:19 For it pleased the Father that in Him all the fullness should dwell,

Colossians 1:28 Him we preach, warning every man and teaching every man in all wisdom, that we may present every man perfect in Christ Jesus.

Colossians 2:3 in whom are hidden all the treasures of wisdom and knowledge.

Colossians 2:5 For though I am absent in the flesh, yet I am with you in spirit, rejoicing to see your good order and the steadfastness of your faith in Christ.

Colossians 2:6 As you therefore have received Christ Jesus the Lord, so walk in Him,

Colossians 2:7 rooted and built up in Him and established in the faith, as you have been taught, abounding in it with thanksgiving.

Colossians 2:9 For in Him dwells all the fullness of the Godhead bodily;

Colossians 2:10 and you are complete in Him, who is the head of all principality and power.

Colossians 2:11 In Him you were also circumcised with the circumcision made without hands, by putting off the body of the sins of the flesh, by the circumcision of Christ,

Colossians 3:17 And whatever you do in word or deed, do all in the name of the Lord Jesus, giving thanks to God the Father through Him.

1 Thessalonians 2:14 For you, brethren, became imitators of the churches of God which are in Judea in Christ Jesus. For you also suffered the same things from your own countrymen, just as they did from the Judeans,

1 Thessalonians 4:16 For the Lord Himself will descend from heaven with a shout, with the voice of an archangel, and with the trumpet of God. And the dead in Christ will rise first.

1 Thessalonians 5:18 in everything give thanks; for this is the will of God in Christ Jesus for you.

2 Thessalonians 1:12 that the name of our Lord Jesus Christ may be glorified in you, and you in Him, according to the grace of our God and the Lord Jesus Christ.

1 Timothy 1:14 And the grace of our Lord was exceedingly abundant, with faith and love which are in Christ Jesus.

1 Timothy 2:7 for which I was appointed a preacher and an apostle—I am speaking the truth in Christ and not lying—a teacher of the Gentiles in faith and truth.

1 Timothy 3:13 For those who have served well as deacons obtain for themselves a good standing and great boldness in the faith which is in Christ Jesus.

2 Timothy 1:1 Paul, an apostle of Jesus Christ by the will of God, according to the promise of life which is in Christ Jesus,

2 Timothy 1:9 who has saved us and called us with a holy calling, not according to our works, but according to His own purpose and grace which was given to us in Christ Jesus before time began,

2 Timothy 1:13 Hold fast the pattern of sound words which you have heard from me, in faith and love which are in Christ Jesus.

2 Timothy 2:1 You therefore, my son, be strong in the grace that is in Christ Jesus.

2 Timothy 2:10 Therefore I endure all things for the sake of the elect, that they also may obtain the salvation which is in Christ Jesus with eternal glory.

2 Timothy 3:12 Yes, and all who desire to live godly in Christ Jesus will suffer persecution.

2 Timothy 3:15 and that from childhood you have known the Holy Scriptures, which are able to make you wise for salvation through faith which is in Christ Jesus.

Philemon 1:6 that the sharing of your faith may become effective by the acknowledgment of every good thing which is in you in Christ Jesus.

Philemon 1:8 Therefore, though I might be very bold in Christ to command you what is fitting,

Philemon 1:23 Epaphras, my fellow prisoner in Christ Jesus, greets you,

Hebrews 1:2 has in these last days spoken to us by His Son, whom He has appointed heir of all things, through whom also He made the worlds;

Hebrews 2:10 For it was fitting for Him, for whom are all things and by whom are all things, in bringing many sons to glory, to make the captain of their salvation perfect through sufferings.

Hebrews 7:25 Therefore He is also able to save to the uttermost those who come to God through Him, since He always lives to make intercession for them.

1 Peter 1:21 who through Him believe in God, who raised Him from the dead and gave Him glory, so that your faith and hope are in God.

1 Peter 3:16 having a good conscience, that when they defame you as evildoers, those who revile your good conduct in Christ may be ashamed.

1 Peter 5:14 Greet one another with a kiss of love. Peace to you all who are in Christ Jesus. Amen.

2 Peter 1:17 For He received from God the Father honor and glory when such a voice came to Him from the Excellent Glory: "This is My beloved Son, in whom I am well pleased."

1 John 2:5 But whoever keeps His word, truly the love of God is perfected in him. By this we know that we are in Him.

1 John 2:6 He who says he abides in Him ought himself also to walk just as He walked.

1 John 2:27 But the anointing which you have received from Him abides in you, and you do not need that anyone teach you; but as the same anointing teaches you concerning all things, and is true, and is not a lie, and just as it has taught you, you will abide in Him.

1 John 2:28 And now, little children, abide in Him, that when He appears, we may have confidence and not be ashamed before Him at His coming.

1 John 3:6 Whoever abides in Him does not sin. Whoever sins has neither seen Him nor known Him.

1 John 3:24 Now he who keeps His commandments abides in Him, and He in him. And by this we know that He abides in us, by the Spirit whom He has given us.

1 John 4:9 In this the love of God was manifested toward us, that God has sent His only begotten Son into the world, that we might live through Him.

1 John 4:13 By this we know that we abide in Him, and He in us, because He has given us of His Spirit.

1 John 4:15 Whoever confesses that Jesus is the Son of God, God abides in him, and he in God.

1 John 4:16 And we have known and believed the love that God has for us. God is love, and he who abides in love abides in God, and God in him.

1 John 5:20 And we know that the Son of God has come and has given us an understanding, that we may know Him who is true; and we are in Him who is true, in His Son Jesus Christ. This is the true God and eternal life.

# About the Author

Dr. Al Jennings is the Senior Pastor of Summit Church and the CEO of Summit Ministries International. He has a B.S. degree from Ball State University and a Th.D from Life Christian University.

Dr. Jennings travels throughout the United States and internationally ministering the gospel of Jesus Christ. His purpose is to teach people how to win in life through an understanding of God's unconditional love and grace. He wants people to know that God is a good God and that He's not mad at them; He's madly in love with them.

Dr. Jennings is the author of *Unlocking the Mystery of Tongues, God Wants You Healed, Basic Training for Victorious Christian Living, and God is Not Mad at You; He's Madly in Love with You.*

www.aljennings.com